my name is not
Isabella

story by Jennifer Fosberry • pictures by Mike Litwin

SCHOLASTIC INC.

For Toots, who was always *"one of those women,"* and for my kids, Bella, Gus, and Sera, may you be whatever you want to be. **—JF**

For Arijá and Lydia—never let anyone tell you what you can't do—and for Isabella, a very brave little girl. **—ML**

No part of this publication may be reproduced, stored in a retrieval system, or transmitted in any form or by any means, electronic, mechanical, photocopying, recording, or otherwise, without written permission of the publisher. For information regarding permission, write to Sourcebooks Jabberwocky, an imprint of Sourcebooks, Inc., P.O. Box 4410, Naperville, IL 60567-4410.

ISBN 978-0-545-53546-5

Copyright © 2008, 2010 by Jennifer Fosberry.
Cover and internal illustrations copyright © Mike Litwin.
Cover and internal design copyright © 2010 by Sourcebooks, Inc.
All rights reserved. Published by Scholastic Inc., 557 Broadway, New York, NY 10012, by arrangement with Sourcebooks Jabberwocky, an imprint of Sourcebooks, Inc.
SCHOLASTIC and associated logos are trademarks and/or registered trademarks of Scholastic Inc.

12 11 10 9 8 7 6 5 4 3 2 1   13 14 15 16 17 18/0

Printed in the U.S.A.

This edition first printing, January 2013

40

"Good morning, *Isabella*," the mother said.

"It's time to get up and out of bed."

"My name is not Isabella!" said the little girl.

"Then who has been sleeping in my daughter's bed?" asked the mother.

"I am SALLY,

the greatest, toughest astronaut who ever was!"

"Well, Sally, **BLAST** out of bed, put on your space suit and come downstairs for breakfast."

"Good morning, Sally,"
the mother said. "It's time
for breakfast, pull up a chair."

"My name is not Sally!"
said the little girl.

"Then who will eat this
fine breakfast I cooked?"
asked the mother.

"I am **ANNIE**, the greatest, fastest sharpshooter who ever was!"

"Well, Annie, **RIDE** on over here and eat up. These are some fine vittles and every cowgirl needs a proper meal."

"Okay, Annie," the mother said.
"It's time for school."

My name is not Annie!
said the little girl.

"Then who will go outside
and wait for the bus?"
asked the mother.

bravest activist who ever was!"

"Well, Rosa, MARCH out there and take your seat on the bus."

"Welcome home, Rosa," the mother said. "Did you have a nice day at school?"

My name is not Rosa!" said the little girl.

"Then who will eat these
cookies I made while she
does her homework?"
asked the mother.

"I am **MARIE**, the greatest, smartest scientist who ever was!"

$CO + OK_3 = IE^2$

CO_2

"Well, Marie, sit down and **DISCOVER** the answers to your homework, and I will get the cookies."

"Time for dinner, Marie," the mother said. "Come help me set the table."

"My name is not Marie!" said the little girl.

"Then who will help me set out the dishes for our fine meal?" asked the mother.

"I am ELIZABETH, the greatest, kindest doctor who ever was!"

"Well, Elizabeth, have PATIENCE with your mother and use the nice plates, please."

"It's almost bedtime, Elizabeth," the mother said. "Come upstairs and take your bath."

"My name is not Elizabeth!" said the little girl.

"Then who will relax in this nice hot bath I have drawn?" asked the mother.

"I am *Mommy*, the greatest, sweetest mother who ever was!"

"Well, Mommy, get in the bathtub. I hope you *love* the bubbles."

When the little girl climbed into bed, the mother said, "Good night, Mommy."

"My name is not Mommy!"
said the little girl.

"Then who will be sleeping in my daughter's bed tonight?" asked the mother.

"It's me, *Isabella*, the sweetest, kindest, smartest, bravest, fastest, toughest, greatest girl that ever was," said the little girl as she fell asleep and dreamed about who she would be...

...*tomorrow.*

women who changed the world

SALLY RIDE (1951-):

Sally Ride was the first woman from the United States to travel to space. She studied physics at Stanford University. In 1978, Sally was one of six women to join NASA and train for space missions. On June 18, 1983, she flew on the space shuttle *Challenger*. Her job was to test a robot arm. Since then Sally has been a teacher at many California universities. She has started many programs to help kids become more interested in math, science, and technology.

An **ASTRONAUT** is a person who does their work in space. There are different jobs on the spacecraft. Some people are pilots. Some people fix the spacecraft. Some people do science research.

ANNIE OAKLEY (1860-1926):

Annie Oakley was one of the first women superstars. When she was young, her family was poor. For many years, she had to live away from home at a poor farm. She also lived with another family and worked as a servant. When she came home her family was about to lose their farm. Annie hunted for small game and sold it to the local town. When she was fifteen, she paid all the money for her mother's house. Many people knew she was a very good shooter. When Frank Butler, a famous marksman, visited her town, he challenged anyone to a shooting contest. Annie won the prize and later married Frank. One time Annie filled in for Frank's shooting show. Annie and Frank soon realized that she was much better at the show, so she became the star. Annie traveled throughout America and Europe, performing with "Buffalo Bill's Wild West" show. Annie told people that she fought to be able to compete and perform as a woman. She also told them that she always dressed and acted like a lady.

A **SHARPSHOOTER** is a person who can shoot a gun and hit a target many times and very accurately.

ROSA PARKS (1913-2005):

Rosa Parks was a civil rights activist. She lived in Montgomery, Alabama, at a time when people of color were not treated the same as white people. They were made to sit in different areas in restaurants and buses. They had to use different bathrooms, drinking fountains, and even schools. Rosa and her husband did not think this was right. They belonged to a group called the National Association for the Advancement of Colored People (NAACP) that was trying to change things. On December 1, 1955, Rosa was riding the bus home from work. She was told to give up her seat for a white person. She refused. The bus driver had her arrested. This event brought all the black people of Montgomery together. They decided not to ride the bus until the laws were changed. This boycott lasted more than a year. The Supreme Court made a decision against the Montgomery rule and outlawed separate areas for different people on buses and trains. For the rest of her life, Rosa worked to teach about equal rights for all people.

An **ACTIVIST** is a person who fights for what they believe through protests, teaching, speeches, and other means.

MARIE CURIE (1867–1934):

Marie Curie was a scientist who first learned how radiation works. She was born in Warsaw, Poland. Her parents were teachers and wanted her to go to school. The Russians were in charge of Warsaw then and did not allow the Polish people to learn science. Marie wanted to go to school in France but her family did not have much money. Marie worked as a nanny and used her money to send her older sister to school. When her sister finished her schooling, it was Marie's turn. She moved to Paris and went to the Sorbonne. She studied math and physics. She met her husband at school and they worked together doing research. Their work led to the discovery of two new elements. The elements were named radium and polonium. Because of their work, people began to understand radioactivity. Marie said that the radiation energy came from inside the atoms. Marie was the first woman awarded a Nobel Prize and the first woman to teach at the Sorbonne.

A **SCIENTIST** is a person who tries to understand and explain how things work. They may study animals, machines, or rocks.

ELIZABETH BLACKWELL (1821–1910):

Elizabeth Blackwell was the first woman to go to school to become a doctor. She decided that she wanted to be a doctor after a sick friend said she was sad there were no women doctors to treat her. Elizabeth applied to more than twenty-five schools that said no to her. Finally, Geneva College in New York said they would accept her if all her male classmates would agree. They may have thought it was a joke, but they said yes. Elizabeth finished first in her class in January 1849. She moved to France to practice. One day when she was giving eye medicine to a baby, an accident happened. Elizabeth lost her sight in one eye. Now she could not be a surgeon. Elizabeth went back to the United States but she still could not get a job as a doctor. Elizabeth opened a clinic for poor women and children that could not go to other doctors. She also started a medical school for women to learn to be doctors.

A **DOCTOR** is a person who knows how the body works. They help people who are hurt or sick. Doctors try to keep people healthy.

MOMMY:

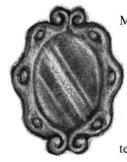

Mommy was once a little girl with a big imagination and big dreams. Mommy imagined growing up to be a princess, a firefighter, a dancer, an engineer, a teacher, a journalist, a professional roller skater, and more. She dreamed about having wonderful children and being a great mother. Now she is a wonderful mom and still has a big imagination. Mommy loves her children and gives them snuggly hugs. She is smart and funny and tells great stories.

A **MOTHER** is a person who uses love and wisdom to raise children to be caring, accomplished adults.

acknowledgments

I would like to thank all the women who strived to make changes in the world and allow me so many opportunities. I am grateful to my husband and family for always believing it could happen. **—JF**

list of works consulted

on these and other exciting women check out the following:

BOOKS:

Adler, David and Robert Casilla (illustrator). *A Picture Book of Rosa Parks.* New York: Holiday House, 1993.

Bennett, William J. (editor) and Michael Hague (illustrator). *The Children's Book of Heroes.* New York: Simon & Schuster Children's Publishing, 1997.

Cheney, Lynne and Robin Preiss Glasser (illustrator). *A is for Abigail: An Almanac of Amazing American Women.* New York: Simon & Schuster Children's Publishing, 2003.

Chin-Lee, Cynthia, Megan Helsy (illustrator), and Sean Addy (illustrator). *Amelia to Zora: Twenty-Six Women Who Changed the World.* Watertown, MA: Charlesbridge Publishing, 2005.

Giovanni, Nikki and Bryan Collier (illustrator). *Rosa.* New York: Henry Holt & Company, 2005.

Gray, Gwendolyn. *Girls Who Grew Up Great: A Book of Encouragement for Girls about Amazing Women Who Dared to Dream.* Boulder, CO: Blue Mountain Press, 2003.

Kishel, Ann-Marie. *Elizabeth Blackwell: A Life of Diligence.* Pull Ahead Books. Minneapolis: Lerner Publications Company, 2007.

Krensky, Stephen and Bernie Fuchs (illustrator). *Shooting for the Moon: The Amazing Life and Times of Annie Oakley.* New York: Farrar, Straus & Giroux, 2001.

Krull, Kathleen and Kathryn Hewitt (illustrator). *Lives of Extraordinary Women: Rulers, Rebels (and What the Neighbors Thought).* New York: Harcourt Children's Books, 2000.

Macy, Sue. *Bull's-Eye: A Photobiography of Annie Oakley.* Washington, DC: National Geographic Children's Books, 2006.

Mader, Jan. *Elizabeth Blackwell.* First Biographies. Mankato, MN: Capstone Press, 2007.

McDounough, Yona Zeldis, and Mallah Zeldis (illustrator). *Sisters in Strength: American Women Who Made a Difference.* New York: Henry Holt & Company, 2000.

Nichols, Catherine. *Sally Ride.* Scholastic News Nonfiction Readers. New York: Children's Press, 2005.

Parks, Rosa, Jim Haskins, and Wil Clay. *I Am Rosa Parks.* Easy to Read. New York: Puffin, 1997.

Rau, Dana Meachen. *Marie Curie.* Compass Point Early Biographies. Mankato, MN. Compass Point Books, 2000.

Raum, Elizabeth. *Sally Ride.* American Lives. Portsmouth, NH: Heinemann, 2005.

Ride, Sally. *To Space and Back.* New York: Lothrop, Lee & Shepard Books, 1986.

Schaefer, Wyatt S. *Marie Curie.* First Biographies. Mankato, MN: Capstone Press, 2004.

Steele, Philip. *Marie Curie: The Woman Who Changed the Course of Science.* Washington, DC: National Geographic Books, 2006.

Thimmesh, Catherine and Melissa Sweet (illustrator). *Girls Think of Everything: Stories of Ingenious Inventions by Women.* New York: Houghton Mifflin Company, 2000.

Willis, Charles M. *Annie Oakley.* DK Biography. New York: DK Children, 2007.

WEBSITES:

"Annie Oakley." Dorchester Library. www.dorchesterlibrary.org/library/aoakley.html.

"Annie Oakley: She Shot the Ashes Off the Kaiser's Cigaret." Cowgirl's Dream. www.cowgirls.com/dream/cowgals/oakley.htm.

"Biographical Data: Sally Ride." NASA. www.jsc.nasa.gov/Bios/htmlbios/ride-sk.html.

"Black History: Rosa Parks." GALE CENGAGE Learning. www.galegroup.com/free_resources/bhm/bio/parks_r.htm.

"Elizabeth Blackwell." About.com: Women's History. womenshistory.about.com/od/blackwellelizabeth/a/eliz_blackwell.htm.

"Elizabeth Blackwell (1821-1910)." Biography.com. www.biography.com/search/article.do?id=9214198.

"Elizabeth Blackwell, MD." Wellness Directory of Minnesota. www.mnwelldir.org/docs/history/biographies/blackwell.htm.

Info Please: All the Knowledge You Need. www.infoplease.com/people.html.

"Marie Curie." The AIP Center for History of Physics. www.aip.org/history/curie.

"Marie Curie." The Great Idea Finder. www.ideafinder.com/history/inventors/curie.htm.

"Rosa Louise Parks Biography." Rosa & Raymond Parks Institute for Self Development. www.rosaparks.org/bio.html.

"Rosa Parks." Academy of Achievement. www.achievement.org/autodoc/page/par0bio-1.

"Sally Kristen Ride: First American Woman in Space." Lucidcafé Library. www.lucidcafe.com/library/96may/ride.html.

"Women in History: Annie Oakley." Lakewood Public Library. www.lkwdpl.org/wihohio/oakl-ann.htm.

"Women's History: Elizabeth Blackwell." GALE CENGAGE Learning. www.galegroup.com/free_resources/whm/bio/blackwell_e.htm.

"Women's History: Marie Curie." GALE CENGAGE Learning. www.galegroup.com/free_resources/whm/bio/curie_m.htm.